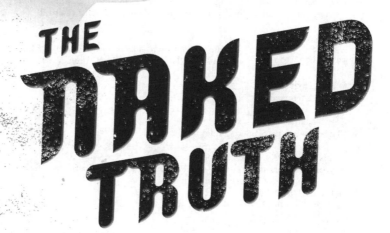

THE NAKED TRUTH

LAKITA GARTH

Regal

From Gospel Light
Ventura, California, U.S.A.

PUBLISHED BY REGAL BOOKS
FROM GOSPEL LIGHT
VENTURA, CALIFORNIA, U.S.A.
PRINTED IN THE U.S.A.

Regal Books is a ministry of Gospel Light, a Christian publisher dedicated to serving
the local church. We believe God's vision for Gospel Light is to provide church leaders
with biblical, user-friendly materials that will help them evangelize, disciple and minister to children, youth and families.

It is our prayer that this Regal book will help you discover biblical truth for your own
life and help you meet the needs of others. May God richly bless you.

*For a free catalog of resources from Regal Books/Gospel Light, please call your Christian supplier
or contact us at* 1-800-4-GOSPEL *or* www.regalbooks.com.

Garth, Lakita.
  The naked truth. Student guide / Lakita Garth.
    p. cm.
  ISBN 0-8307-4330-8 (trade paper)
  1. Sex—Religious aspects—Christianity—Textbooks. 2. Sex instruction for teenagers—
Religious aspects—Christianity. I. Title.
  BT708.G378 2007b
  241'.660835—dc22   2006034972

1   2   3   4   5   6   7   8   9   10   /   10   09   08   07

Rights for publishing this book in other languages are contracted by Gospel Light
Worldwide, the international nonprofit ministry of Gospel Light. Gospel Light Worldwide also provides publishing and technical assistance to international publishers dedicated to producing Sunday School and Vacation Bible School curricula and books in
the languages of the world. For additional information, visit www.gospellightworld
wide.org; write to Gospel Light Worldwide, P.O. Box 3875, Ventura, CA 93006; or send
an e-mail to info@gospellightworldwide.org.

Contents

The Naked Truth

Introduction

For this reason a man will leave his father and mother and be united to his wife, and they will become one flesh. The man and the woman were both naked, and they felt no shame.

—GOD (GENESIS 2:24-25)

Pick almost any movie made for teenagers and adults (PG-13 or R) and you are guaranteed to see someone in bed or in the shower with someone else. Most of us have watched intimate encounters on television and in the movies for much of our lives.

By the time most of us are in high school, we begin to wonder, *What would it be like to have an intense romantic relationship? Will I ever fall in love and have great sex?*

There's a reason sex is such a big part of our culture: God made us not only to want sex but also to enjoy sex for a lifetime.

From the very beginning, God created man and woman to enjoy each other. We were shaped to find pleasure in the opposite sex: their bodies, their minds, and their spiritual lives. We were created to fully know someone and to be fully known.

God's plan for you includes a great, satisfying and—yes!—amazing sex life. Do you want to know God's plan for a great sex life?

The Naked Truth with Lakita

Now it's time to meet Lakita! In each lesson you will have a chance to hear from Lakita Garth, who has lived her life following God's call to abstain from sex until marriage. As you watch this video, write down any questions or thoughts that come to you in the journal space provided below. Enjoy the video!

_____

_____

_____

_____

_____

_____

Take a moment to talk with your leader and others in the group about questions and comments you have after watching the video.

The Hook-Up

Whether we realize it or not, all of us have an opinion about sex. Below are some typical comments you might hear people say about sex before marriage:

- "Other people may contract a sexually transmitted disease, but it won't happen to me; I'll be careful."
- "Sex is just for having babies, it's not something to enjoy."
- "Oral sex and touching are a safe way to show love physically without actually having sex."
- "Condoms are the best way to practice safe sex."
- "If I've already had sex, there's really no good reason to not have sex before marriage since I'm no longer a virgin."
- "If I'm dating the person I know I'm going to marry, then it's okay to have sex because they will eventually be my spouse."
- "Everybody, except for really religious or ugly people, enjoy sex."
- "Sex just happens."

Are these statements, ideas and assumptions true? Yes, no, maybe? The problem with discovering truth is that sometimes a lie wears a mask that looks a lot like the face of truth. In fact, a really good lie needs to have some truth in order for it to be believable.

Check out the situations below and think about what seems true and what seems like a lie.

Situation #1

Bobby and Sharon were celebrating their one-month anniversary since they began dating. One night, after going to see a movie, Sharon told Bobby that her roommate had gone home for the weekend and that they had her dorm room to themselves. Bobby and Sharon started making out and pretty soon found themselves wanting to go all the way. Sharon said they had better not because she didn't want to get pregnant. Bobby said, "We won't do this all the time. We love each other and this is our anniversary. After all, it's not likely that you'll get pregnant if we do it just once. It can't happen to us."

What seems true about Bobby's opinion?

_____

_____

_____

_____

What seems untrue about his opinion?

_____

_____

_____

_____

Situation #2

Katrina had lots of questions about sex. She had just attended a Christian retreat with her church group and the speaker told them to "just say no to sex." In fact, he told them that listening to hip hop, watching music videos and viewing R-rated movies was evil. The problem was, Katrina was curious about sex even though she knew that God intended for her to wait until she was married. So, she talked to her older cousin, Regina, who was living with her boyfriend. Regina laughed when Katrina told her about the guest speaker at the retreat. Regina pointed out, "Having sex before you are married prepares you to have a better and more satisfying sex life with your future spouse because you have more practice."

What seems true about Regina's opinion?

_____

_____

_____

_____

What seems untrue about Regina's opinion?

_____

_____

_____

_____

Everyone has an opinion about sex. Many of us grow up in church learning that sex before marriage is wrong, yet most of the time it's never explained *why* it's wrong. Sex and drugs are often under the category of "just say no." If our parents are single and have an active dating life, we might learn that sex outside of marriage is acceptable, as long as "you love each other," are in a "committed relationship" or if you do it "responsibly."

How do you know what's really true about sex?

That's what we are going to be studying for the next eight weeks. You are going to learn to know the difference between truths and lies that are wrapped in truth's clothing to deceive people.

Now let's take a look at a couple of stories from the Bible in which someone needed to decide the difference between the truth and a lie.

The Gospel Truth

What would paradise look like to you? How about eating all the food you want, having great weather, walking close with God, and being able to run around completely naked with the person created especially for you? In fact, you would feel so loved and accepted by God and the other person that you would not feel any sense of embarrassment or shame. Well, that's what it was like for the first man and woman.

Everything was perfect. But even in paradise the man and the woman were tempted to turn away from God. Every day they could choose to enjoy the great life they had been given or they could choose to pursue what seemed like a greater pleasure. God loved the man and woman so much that He gave them a warning. Like a parent who warns their children of possible dangers, God warned the first humans about what not to do in their own little paradise.

Read Genesis 2:16-17.

Write in your own words how God described what was good and what was dangerous about life on Earth.

_____

_____

_____

_____

_____

_____

_____

_____

Even though God told the man and the woman the truth, they began to question whether what God said was completely true. In fact, the woman began to talk to the greatest deceiver of all time. The ancients described the "great liar" as a serpent. Jesus called him Satan. Eve was deceived into thinking that Satan had her best interests at heart and that God was keeping her from pleasure. Satan dressed up a lie to look like truth and the results were disastrous.

Read Genesis 3:1-7.

What lie did the serpent tell the man and woman that may have seemed true but, in fact, destroyed their paradise?

_____

_____

_____

_____

_____

Read Genesis 3:6 again and describe the emotions you think the man and woman were feeling when they were faced with the decision to follow God's plan or to follow their passions.

_____

_____

_____

_____

_____

What did they feel after they ate the "forbidden fruit"? Why do you think they felt that way?

_____

_____

_____

_____

Read Genesis 3:8-20.

How many consequences can you discover that the man and woman experienced as a result of choosing not to abstain from the forbidden fruit?

_____

_____

_____

_____

God commanded the man and woman to abstain from eating the fruit of the tree of the knowledge of good and evil. God knew that if they ate from that particular tree, they would face some real and grave consequences. Unfortunately, the man and woman ignored the warning and chose another option that brought about some pretty devastating results. They chose to believe a lie that looked a lot like truth.

The Gospel Truth: Undressing Satan's Lies

In the video, Lakita tells the story of two characters: Truth and Lie. At the end of the story she describes how each of us are going to be faced with the same challenge the town's people faced: Are you going to believe a lie in truth's clothing or the Naked Truth?

In The Gospel Truth section, we saw the devastating consequences of Adam and Eve's choice to believe the lie in truth's clothing. Fortunately, Scripture does not just give us examples of people who failed but also of people who succeeded.

Did you know that even Jesus had to decide whether He wanted to follow God or not? It's true! Jesus was just as human as you and me and at some point He decided to follow God's call. It all began when He was baptized. After His baptism, He had to decide whether He was going to believe a lie in truth's clothing or believe God's truth.

Read Matthew 4:1-17.

Satan sometimes uses the Bible to dress up his lies with truth. But the Bible is *God's* truth. The words of Scripture tell us what God wants for our lives. God loves you so much that He gave you a book to show you how to have the best life ever. (Some people say BIBLE stands for Basic Instructions Before Leaving Earth.) As you read this passage, notice how Satan dressed up a lie to make it look like truth, and how Jesus undressed the lie to expose the truth.

Lie #1: We Need to Satisfy Our Every Desire (Self-Control)
Read Matthew 4:1-4.

Let's face it: After 40 days of fasting in the wilderness, anyone would be starving. Satan knew that Jesus had huge physical needs, so he tempted Him with His deepest desire at that moment: food!

Satan's first lie was that if our physical needs are met, then we will be happy.

How did Satan dress this lie up as truth?

_____

_____

_____

_____

How did Jesus undress this lie of Satan? (Check out Deuteronomy 8:3.)

_____

_____

_____

_____

God is more than able to provide for our physical needs, but
there is something more important: following God's commands.
When we follow the way God calls us to live, we experience God's
greatest gifts.

In the DVD, the first character trait that gave Lakita and
her brothers the ability to make good decisions is self-control.
Jesus practiced self-control by refusing to use His powers to
turn stone into bread when He was hungry in the desert. By
abstaining from bread, Jesus chose to put God's commands
before His physical needs.

What would have been wrong if Jesus had made all the bread
He wanted and followed Satan's lie?

_____

_____

_____

In what areas of your life do you wish you had more self-control?

_____

_____

_____

_____

_____

Lie #2: God Will Protect Us Even When We Do Something Stupid (Self-Discipline)

Read Matthew 4:5-6.

Satan then pulled out another lie: If Jesus was really God's Son, then He could do what He wanted and God would save Him.

We often do things against God's will and then get mad at God for not protecting us. If we have sex, we think, *No problem. God won't let me get an STD or get pregnant. After all, God loves me!*

Wrong! God *does* love you, but you are still responsible for your actions.

Read Psalm 91:11-12.

How did Satan dress this lie up with the truth?

_____

_____

_____

How did Jesus undress the lie? (Check out Deuteronomy 6:16.)

_____

_____

_____

To put God to a test is to do something to prove that *God will follow your* commands.

Satan knew that God would protect Jesus from physical harm. After all, God's plan for Jesus was that He would teach, draw others into a relationship with God, and die on the cross to save humanity. God would never allow Jesus to get hurt; Satan knew it and Jesus knew it.

So why didn't Jesus just prove God's power and follow Satan's request? Jesus didn't go along with Satan's scheme because He had nothing to prove. Jesus disciplined Himself to follow God because He really did not care about what Satan thought or wanted. When you know the truth, you won't have to prove yourself to others, just like Jesus didn't have to prove Himself to Satan.

In what ways do you see people putting God to a test?

_____

_____

_____

_____

The second character trait that had an impact on Lakita's life is self-discipline. She knew the truth and the truth helped her and her brothers to stay focused on their goals. Choosing to follow God's plan for sex and choosing to be disciplined enough to follow your belief are giant steps toward experiencing an amazing sex life.

Lie #3: The Fastest Way Is the Best Way
(Delayed Gratification)

Satan told Jesus that He could have everything if He would bow down and worship Satan instead of God. God's long-term plan for Jesus also offered Him everything—eventually to become "top dog" of the world. The only problem with God's plan was that it included waiting, serving and dying on a cross. It meant that Jesus would have to sacrifice a lot in order to have God's best (see Philippians 2:5-11). Satan, on the other hand, said, "You don't have to wait. You can have all of it right now. Just turn away from God and follow me."

It's often a lot easier to bow down in the moment and to accept Satan's offer of immediate gratification than it is to wait. Lie number three, then, is that we can take the easy way and still have God's best.

How did Jesus address Satan differently in order to undress this truth?

_____

_____

_____

_____

What did God do for Jesus after He survived this test?

_____

_____

_____

Jesus decided to follow God's way of sacrifice instead of satisfying Himself. Just like with Jesus, God's plan for your life may require you to delay immediate pleasures in order to gain something better down the road.

That's what abstinence is all about. It's not saying no for the sake of saying no. It's saying no because there is something better in the end. The Bible speaks clearly about sex. Say no before you are married so that someday you'll be able to say yes for a lifetime—to your spouse.

Doing the Truth

In the video, Lakita explains that the decision to remain abstinent until marriage can be made based on the same decision-making process used to achieve your goals in other areas of life. The way to make a good choice is condensed in these four steps:

1. Know your options and know the consequences.
2. Make a decision. Choose an option and set a goal.
3. Find others who will support you.
4. Plan and take practical steps to achieve your goal.

Now as a group, choose a decision that every high school person must make. Then work through how you might go about making the decision based on the decision-making process outlined above.

Step 1: Know your options and know the consequences.
List four options for making this particular decision and the possible consequences.

For example: *Going to prom.*

Options:	Consequences:
a. *Ask someone out*	*Request rejected*
b. *Ask someone out*	*Request accepted*
c. *Not go at all*	*Feel lonely and left out*
d. *Go with friends*	*Have low-pressure fun*

Step 2: Make a decision. Choose an option and set a goal.
Of the four options, choose which option would be the best and set the goal you would like to achieve.

Option:	Goal:
Ask someone out.	*Find a date by the end of the week.*

Step 3: Find others who will support you.
Make a list of the group of friends and adults who you will ask to support you in this decision.

Best friends

_____

_____

_____

_____

Parents

_____

_____

_____

Youth group members

_____

_____

_____

Step 4: Plan and take practical steps to achieve your goal.
List three actions you will take this week that will help you follow
through on your decision.

1. *Find the best looking guy/girl in your school.*
2. *Ask that person to talk after school.*
3. *Ask that person out.*

The Big Finish

We've covered a lot of material today. Basically, we've looked at
three important points to help you discover God's incredible
plan for your life:

1. God loves you and wants the best for you. He's given
   you the freedom to choose to follow Him.

2. Three character traits of self-control, self-discipline
   and delayed gratification offer you more tools to experience God's best for your life.

3. *The Naked Truth* is about you having an amazing sex
   life. Abstinence education is about preparing you to
   have the best sex and to enjoy it for a lifetime.

It Can't Happen to Me

Introduction

When we first sit behind the steering wheel of a car, we usually feel like our stomach is tied up in knots. We flip-flop between terror and excitement. After a while, though, when we have some experience driving, the fear and excitement wear off. And when driving becomes routine, we may even begin to take dangerous chances.

We eat, talk on our cell phones, try to find our favorite CD, and talk to our friend in the next seat, all while driving on busy streets without giving it much thought. Somewhere in the back of our minds we know that accidents happen, but we think that they would never happen to us because we are in control, and then . . . BAM!!!

We look up from our CD player, drop our cell phone, spill our soda, only to discover we've rear-ended the car in front of us. At first we blame everyone else, but in reality, we weren't paying attention. We thought we had everything under control. We ignored the possible negative consequences of our decisions and ended up paying for it.

What we thought could never happen to us . . . happened.

The same thing can happen when we begin dating. At first we're excited and nervous and we try to do everything right. We've heard for years that we should not have sex because we risk getting pregnant or getting infected with a sexually transmitted disease, like herpes or gonorrhea. But after a while, we have our first kiss. Then, kissing eventually leads to touching. Touching quickly proceeds to . . . well, you get the picture.

We look around at our friends who are having sex and most of them aren't pregnant and no one ever talks about having an STD. Sure, some get pregnant—but we tell ourselves that they took too many chances. That won't happen to us because we'll be careful.

Why not have sex? After all, getting pregnant or getting an STD won't happen to me.

Remember how Jesus undressed Satan's lie in lesson one? In this study we are going to undress the lie that says "It can't happen to me." We will:

1. Take an honest look at the consequences of sex before marriage

2. Think through how we can decrease our vulnerability to those consequences

3. Study God's Word to understand the plan He has laid out for us to enjoy the best sex possible and to enjoy it for a lifetime

Before jumping into the lesson, take some time to pray and ask that God would give you wisdom to understand His will for your life.

Now, let's do a quick review from last week's lesson.

The Naked Truth with Lakita

The affair of David and Bathsheba happened around 1000 B.C. That's about 3,000 years ago. Over the past 3,000 years, many things have changed, but one thing hasn't changed: People still believe the lie "It can't happen to me."

Sit back and get ready for Lakita to bring this problem to the present. As you watch the video, write down questions or thoughts in the journal space provided. As you watch the video, be sure to write down any thoughts and questions you have while

Lakita talks. Take a moment to talk with the group about your questions and thoughts after watching the video.

_____

_____

_____

_____

_____

If you were offered a choice between drinking from a fresh bottle of water or a bottle that had been used by four strangers, which would you choose?

_____

_____

_____

_____

How did you feel when you heard the story of Nushan Williams?

_____

_____

_____

_____

_____

The Hook-Up

"Stay away from the stove, it's hot!"
   "Don't cross the street; it's dangerous!"
   "Don't talk to strangers!"
   "Don't have sex before marriage!"

People have been telling us *not to do things* our entire lives. As kids, hearing "because I told you so" or fearing punishment from our parents kept us mostly in line. But as we get older, we want to find things out for ourselves. We become like Adam and Eve in the garden. We wonder, *Do I really have to be afraid?*

God gave us curiosity, and exploring the world around us is a gift. God also gave us a brain and His Word so that we can safely explore within the boundaries He set in place. We can enjoy life and not suffer negative consequences if we honor His plans for us.

So how much do you know about the real consequences of sex? Take the quiz below and find out! This is the first step in undressing the lie "It can't happen to me." You might be surprised at just how vulnerable you are.

Sexual Consequences I.Q. Test

Circle one answer for each question below.

1. How many people a day get a sexually transmitted disease?
   a. 100
   b. 5,600
   c. 15,800
   d. 42,000
   e. 120,000

2. In any given year, how many new cases of sexually transmitted diseases are reported?
   a. 500,000
   b. 1 million
   c. 10 million
   d. 12 million
   e. 15 million

3. What percentage of people who contract an STD are high school and college students?
   a. 10%
   b. 25%
   c. 50%
   d. 66%
   e. 93%

4. People who have a sexually transmitted disease always know they have one.
   a. True
   b. False

5. Which causes more deaths worldwide?
   a. Hepatitis B
   b. AIDS

6. STDs cannot be transferred through oral sex.
   a. True
   b. False

7. How many girls over the age of 12 are living with herpes?
   a. 1 in 1,000
   b. 1 in 500
   c. 1 in 100
   d. 1 in 10
   e. 1 in 5

8. How many guys in high school who are sexually active will have at least one STD?
   a. 1 in 1,000
   b. 1 in 500

    c. 1 in 100

    d. 1 in 10

    e. 1 in 4

9. One in three girls will be pregnant at least once before the age of 20.

    a. True

    b. False

10. If you are a Christian who is sexually active, you are less likely than a non-Christian to get pregnant or contract an STD.

    a. True

    b. False

Before we look at the answers to this survey, let's take a look at a great man who experienced some severe negative consequences when he took sex into his own hands.

The Gospel Truth

It seems like every other week a well-known celebrity or person in power gets caught with their pants down by the media.

Do you think Kobe Bryant—one of the highest paid and most popular basketball players for the Los Angeles Lakers—thought he would face rape charges after he slept with a 19-year-old in Colorado? Do you think Bill Clinton thinks that his moments of pleasure with a White House intern were worth facing impeachment as president of the United States?

Many people with money, power and fame believe the lie "It can't happen to me" because these things give them a feeling of invincibility. They think they can beat the odds. You might be surprised to learn that one of the greatest followers of God believed that same lie. Thousands of years later, his story can help us undress Satan's lie.

David loved God. And God loved David so much that He transformed him from a shepherd into the king of the nation of Israel. David's power and greatness caused his enemies to tremble with fear. Throughout his life, David practiced self-control, self-discipline and delayed gratification. David only did as God told him. And God blessed him because of it.

Read 2 Samuel 7:8-17.

Describe how you would feel if you were David and God's prophet Nathan spoke these words to you.

_____

_____

_____

Even great men have times of weakness. David is no different than you or me. For a few moments of sexual pleasure, David decided to play the odds and believe the lie "It can't happen to me."

Read 2 Samuel 11:1-5.

Describe David's feelings when he found out that Bathsheba had become pregnant.

_____

_____

_____

If you became pregnant, or were responsible for a pregnancy, what thoughts and fears would you have?

_____

_____

_____

Read 2 Samuel 11:6-27.

In ancient Israel, the consequence of sleeping with your neighbor's wife was death (see Leviticus 20:10). Even the king of Israel could be killed for adultery. Instead of facing the death penalty—which he deserved by law—David tried to get rid of the problem.

How did David try to get rid of the unwanted pregnancy? Why didn't it work?

_____

_____

_____

_____

Read Exodus 20:1-17 and decide how many of the Ten Commandments David disobeyed.

_____

_____

_____

_____

Read 2 Samuel 12:1-13.

Did God allow David's sin to remain a secret? Make a list of the consequences David faced.

_____

_____

_____

How did God respond to David's acknowledgment of his sin?

_____

_____

_____

Doing the Truth

If you are sleeping with someone, you are sleeping with every person that person has ever slept with and are at risk for every STD that might have been passed on.

The activity below will help you understand the consequences of choosing to give up your virginity.

Your group leader will give you a card that either says "virgin," "sexually active with an STD" or "sexually active with no STD." Follow your leader's instructions to find out who is safe from STDs.

When the game is complete, look around to see who is still sitting. Only the people who remained virgins are guaranteed to have avoided an STD or pregnancy. Take a look at the Sexual Exposure Chart:

Number of Sexual Partners	Number of People Exposed
1	1
2	3
3	7
4	15
5	31
6	63
7	127
8	255
9	511
10	1023
11	2047
12	4095

Note: Data assumes that every person has *only* the same number of partners as you.

Are You as Wise as You Thought?
Let's check out how you did on the Sexual Consequences IQ Test.
Compare your answers to the actual answers below:

1. How many people a day get a sexually transmitted
    disease?
    Answer: d. 42,000

2. In any given year, how many new cases of sexually
    transmitted diseases are reported?
    Answer: e. 15,000,000

3. What percentage of the people who contract STDs
    are high school and college students?
    Answer: d. 66%

4. People who have a sexually transmitted disease always
    know they have one.
    Answer: b. False

5. Which causes more deaths worldwide?
    Answer: a. Hepatitis B

6. STDs cannot be transferred through oral sex.
    Answer: b. False

7. How many girls over age 12 are living with herpes?
    Answer: e. 1 in 5

8. How many guys in high school who are sexually active
    will have at least one STD?
    Answer: e. 1 in 4

9. One in three women will be pregnant at least once before the age of 20.
   Answer: a. True

10. If you are a Christian who is sexually active, you are less likely than a non-Christian to get pregnant or contract an STD.
    Answer: b. False

Sex has consequences. If you choose to wait to have sex until marriage, one consequence could be a lifetime of amazing sex. If you choose to have sex outside of marriage, a one consequence could be an STD or pregnancy. Do you think it could happen to you?

As it ended up, David was responsible for Bathsheba's pregnancy. We saw how fear guided him to make some life-changing decisions with disastrous results. Did you notice that David made all these decisions without Bathsheba's input? This was another poor choice. When a woman becomes pregnant, the man and the woman have to make choices together.

The Big Finish

What stands out to you from the stories of David/Bathsheba?

_____

_____

_____

_____

What surprised you from today's lesson?

_____

_____

_____

Over the next six lessons you will use the T-Chart (see below) to help keep track of what we are learning in each lesson. Each week you'll make an entry about the negative consequences for having sex, e.g., high risk of contracting an STD and significant risk of becoming pregnant. You will also make a list of the positive consequences of following God and practicing 100 percent abstinence until marriage.

Take a moment to fill in the T-Chart with what you've learned from this lesson.

Negative Consequences	Positive Consequences

America's Most Unwanted

Introduction

In the recent Hollywood resurrection of the '80s television classic *Miami Vice*, Sonny Crockett (played by Colin Farrel) and Rico Tubbs (played by Jamie Foxx) passionately pursue a ruthless drug lord, Archangel de Jesus Montoya-Londono, and his Cuban-Chinese banker, Isabella.

In the midst of the vicious war between drug traffickers and law enforcement, Sonny and Isabella begin a heated romance. The affair begins when the two enjoy his favorite drink, a Mojito, in a Cuban nightclub. After finishing the Mojito, Sonny and Isabella burn up the floor with a Latin dance that fills the air with sexual tension.

As sensual Cuban music wraps itself around their twisting bodies, imagine if film director Michael Mann instructed Sonny to lean over and whisper into Isabella's ear:

"Before we head to the hotel room, I need to let you know that I've just finished my last treatment for genital warts, so I should be all clear. You've got nothing to worry about."

Too much reality for Hollywood? Absolutely. That type of dialogue would never fly in a movie. Nobody wants to hear the words "genital warts" when considering sex.

Yet genital warts is on the top 10 list of the most common sexually transmitted diseases that infect people everyday. Sounds like a lot more people ought to hear the words "genital warts" when considering sex, or the words may be just the beginning of a long and miserable acquaintance.

Remember that the first step in making a wise choice is to know your options and *their consequences.*

In this study, Lakita will introduce to you information on a crime family known as "America's Most Unwanted." By the end of this lesson, you'll probably know more than you ever wanted to know about sexually transmitted diseases. Lakita wants you to know the real dangers of multiple sexual partners (i.e., more than one) and not just the Hollywood illusion.

After all, if you had a friend who was going to do something that put him or her at risk, wouldn't you tell your friend?

Now, let's do a quick review from last week's lesson.

The Naked Truth with Lakita

As you prepare to listen to Lakita, take a moment to pray and ask that God would use this time to help you gain wisdom about the choices you make. Write down any thoughts or questions you have while Lakita talks. Here are a couple of questions to get you thinking:

What information in the video did you find most surprising?

_____

_____

_____

_____

Of all the STDs mentioned, which one would you want to live with? Do you know how to be certain you won't have to?

_____

_____

_____

_____

_____

In this video, you will hear some real stories from people who "sinned against" their bodies and contracted a sexually transmitted disease. After the video is shown, think about the following reflection questions:

How does listening to these testimonies affect how you feel about people who have an STD?

_____

_____

_____

_____

_____

How do you think God feels about the people from the video?

_____

_____

_____

_____

_____

What words of comfort do you think God would say to them?

_____

_____

_____

_____

_____

What words of warning would He say?

_____

_____

_____

_____

The Hook-Up

Describe a decision you have made that put you at risk.

_____

_____

_____

_____

In the situation you described above, if you had a friend or knew an adult who could tell you all the possible negative consequences, would you want to hear from them? Why or why not?

_____

_____

_____

_____

If you knew the possible negative consequences of a particular life choice and your friend was taking a huge risk without even knowing it, would you warn your friend? Why or why not?

_____

_____

_____

_____

The Gospel Truth

If you were alive in the 1990s and watched television, you became familiar with the phrase "Friends don't let friends drive drunk." The point was obvious: If you care about someone, you look out for that person. If you love someone, you warn them of the possible negative consequences of their actions. If you see them heading in the wrong direction, you do whatever it takes to help them make a good decision.

God shows His love for us through warnings, too.

Throughout the Bible, God warns His people against making foolish decisions. God desires that everyone experience a dynamic, passion-filled, abundant life. He even laid out a plan so that we could experience that kind of life, and His Word lets us know the consequences of a bad decision.

When God brought His people out of Egypt, He had a plan for them to be a great nation. Ultimately, it was out of this nation that God would bring the Savior of the world. God had big plans: He gave His people land, success against their enemies and leaders to guide them whenever there was a crisis. God provided everything. In those days, other nations had kings to protect the people, but God's people didn't need a king. They had God.

You can imagine, though, how hard it would be to wait on God for answers when the nations around you had flesh-and-blood kings to give them answers. As it turns out, God's people eventually found themselves tired of waiting. They wanted a real king with whom they could speak openly.

Read 1 Samuel 8:1-4.

What reasons did the elders of Israel give Samuel regarding their desire for a king?

_____

_____

_____

From your perspective, is there anything wrong with wanting to be like everyone else? When could wanting to be like others damage or deepen your relationship with God?

_____

_____

_____

Read 1 Samuel 8:6-9.

How does God respond to the elders' request for a king?

_____

_____

_____

_____

Read 1 Samuel 8:10-21.

If you were one of the elders and you heard all the negative consequences that would result from having a king, would you still
want a king?

_____

_____

_____

_____

Are you the type of person who can learn from just being told
or do you need to experience things for yourself?

_____

_____

_____

_____

Why would God still give the people of Israel a king, even though
He knew a king would not be best for them?

_____

_____

_____

_____

The people of Israel grew tired of being different. At some point, they simply wanted to be like everyone around them. God had delivered them from many battles, but they wanted a king to deliver them. They were tired of following God. They did not want to listen to God's advice or warnings anymore.

In their desire for a king, the Israelites had forgotten one critical fact about God. They forgot that God loved them and wanted what was best for them. If only they had listened to His warning. Are you ready to heed the warnings you have heard about sex?

Doing the Truth

Let's get a little personal. It's time for you to seriously consider what life would be like if you were infected with a sexually transmitted disease.

Let's get started. From one of the magazines, select a picture and develop an STD story about the person. The story should include:

- A description of the STD and its symptoms
- A description of the short- and long-term consequences for the STD
- A description of the treatment
- The person's name and what kind of relationship he or she has with God (e.g., committed to following God, doesn't know God at all, goes to church but that's about it, and so forth.)

If you need help with the details about STDs, refer to the following chart of America's Most Unwanted. After you've created that portion of the STD story, read the situations below and incorporate your answer to the questions into your story.

The Usual Suspects

La Familia Bacterial (Bacterial STDs)

Medea	a.k.a.	Chlamydia
Rhea	a.k.a.	Gonorrhea
Phyllis	a.k.a.	Syphilis
P-Deasy	a.k.a.	PID (Pelvic Inflammatory Disease)

La Familia Viral (Viral STDs)

G-Dub	a.k.a.	Human Papillomavirus (HPV)
Herp	a.k.a.	Herpes
Notorious HIV	a.k.a.	HIV/AIDS

Gangs and Cell Groups

The Crabs	a.k.a.	Pubic Lice
Trixie	a.k.a.	Trichomoniasis

First Situation

Imagine that you are the person with the STD. About three months after the diagnosis and initial treatment, you meet someone new and you begin dating. This time you decide to follow God's plan for marriage and you do not have sex. Six months later, you decide to get married.

Describe how you would explain the STD to your future spouse.

_____

_____

_____

_____

_____

Second Situation

Imagine that the STD story is about the person that you would like to marry. He or she tells you that he or she has an STD.

Describe your feelings and how you would handle the situation.

_____

_____

_____

_____

★　★　★

Describe the feelings you had when you imagined that you were the person with the STD. Now describe your feelings when you imagined that your future spouse had an STD.

_____

_____

_____

_____

How does this activity affect your beliefs about having sex before marriage?

_____

_____

_____

_____

The Big Finish

When God created you, He had a great plan for your life. His plan includes your finding someone to love deeply and passionately for a lifetime. Even though we live in a world filled with disease and circumstances beyond our control, there are choices you can make to experience an amazing sex life. Those choices include NOT having an STD.

Let's review some of the basic information about STDs.

- Many STDs do not have visible signs.
- Some STDs have no cure.
- If you have one STD, you are more susceptible to contracting another one.
- Your risk of getting an STD goes up as you have more sex partners.
- The only way to know for sure if you have an STD is to get tested.

If you have had sex, you might have an STD. Since many STDs can go unnoticed, the only way you can be certain is to get tested. There are treatments available for STDs, but only some STDs are fully curable. For example, bacterial STDs can be treated and cured, whereas viral STDs can sometimes be treated but do not go away completely. A person infected with a viral STD must take the responsibility not to spread the disease. If those with viral STDs knowingly spread the disease, those persons may be at legal risk.

It's worth it to get tested even if you've only had sex once. If you are not sure how to get tested or where to go, talk with an adult you trust.

Though not all treatments for STDs are 100 percent effective, God has the power to heal your body as well as your heart. If you've engaged in sexual activity and you truly want to repent (turn away from that behavior), God offers you complete forgiveness and the opportunity to start over. Getting tested could be a good, practical first step toward repentance.

As you come to the end of this lesson, take some time as a group to complete the following T-Chart to describe the negative

consequences of having sex with more than one partner, and
the positive consequences of living like your body is the temple
of the Holy Spirit.

Negative Consequences	Positive Consequences

I'll Practice Safe Sex

Introduction

On August 25, 2005, the people who lived in the city of New Orleans were preparing for yet another hurricane. Having already caused havoc to the islands in the Gulf of Mexico, the arrival of this category-five hurricane called Katrina had people searching for safety. Some left the city, some found shelter in the Super Dome and some hunkered down in their homes to weather the storm. Although the threat of hurricanes is an annual event for those on the Gulf Coast, no one expected the massive damage that would later be known as one of the worst natural disasters in United States history.

Most people believed the city was safe. Sure, there had been warnings by experts that the levees protecting the city might not withstand the pounding of a huge hurricane, but few actually believed they would break. Everybody felt safe, because the levees had held in the past.

On August 27, 2005, the unthinkable happened: The levees near one of the poorest sections of the city broke, and much of the city was soon under water. New Orleans may never fully recover from the tremendous loss of life and damage to the city.

Unfortunately, the roots of this tragedy are grounded in believing a lie: that the safety of New Orleans and the people who lived there was assured by the levees. Investigations reveal that government officials were told by engineers and experts that the levees were not guaranteed to hold, but most of the populace believed they were safe behind these massive barriers. It's one thing to choose to live dangerously when you know the risk, but it's quite another to be told that you are safe when in reality, you are not.

In this lesson, we are going to undress the lie of "safe sex." The lie goes something like this: If you choose to have sex, you should wear a condom because condoms will protect you from pregnancy. Also, condoms will protect you from HIV/AIDS and other sexually transmitted diseases. Condoms protect you from the negative consequences of sex.

Another part of the lie says that God's call to remain abstinent is outdated. In our technologically advanced world, we no longer have to worry about the negative consequences of sex outside of marriage because condoms and other forms of birth control make it "safe."

A more subtle lie says, "If you love God, He will protect you from disease and life-threatening illness, even when you make choices that put your life in danger."

The Naked Truth with Lakita

Before we hear from Lakita, let's take a short quiz to see how much you know about the reality of safe sex. True or False:

1. Male condoms are effective in preventing the spread of most STDs.
   True   False

2. Female condoms (or pouches) give couples a safe way to have sex without the fear of contracting an STD.
   True   False

3. Because your genitals do not touch each other, oral sex is not really sex.
   True   False

4. If you use a condom correctly and it does not leak, tear or break, you do not have to worry about contracting the most common viral STD: HPV.

   True   False

5. If used effectively and all the time, the use of a condom will protect you from ever getting pregnant.

   True   False

6. Gonorrhea throat infections can occur when people participate in oral sex.

   True   False

7. The only 100 percent sure way to prevent STDs or pregnancy is through abstinence.

   True   False

8. Condom manufacturers assure their customers that if they follow the instructions on the package, their condoms will prevent pregnancy and STDs.

   True   False

9. The only condom that would be completely effective would be a condom that covered your entire body.

   True   False

10. God gave us condoms and contraceptives so that we could have sex and not worry about consequences.

    True   False

During the video, compare your answers to the information you hear from Lakita. Take a moment to ask God to use this time to help you gain wisdom concerning the choices you make

in your life. As you watch the video, be sure to write down your
thoughts and questions.

_____

_____

_____

_____

_____

_____

The Hook-Up

Check out this true story of love, sex and dating:

John and Karen were college students who loved God and loved
each other.[1] They had a strong desire to please God with their
bodies. As they continued to date, the tension between pleasing
God and pleasing themselves sexually intensified. They knew
the dangers of pregnancy and STDs, so they agreed to not have
sex until they were married. By sex, they meant actual intercourse. John and Karen never broke that commitment.

You can imagine how shocked Karen was when she missed
her period. After a couple of weeks of worry, she decided to take
a pregnancy test. The test revealed that she was pregnant. Since
Karen had not been close to another man sexually, John was the
father. Even though Karen was technically still a virgin (no
actual penetration), they simulated sex while just wearing
underwear. They thought everything was "safe" if they didn't
go all the way. They were wrong.

John and Karen spent the next year on a roller coaster of
emotions toward each other and toward God. Why would God
allow this to happen? How could they raise a child when they
were still in college? Did they really love each other enough to
get married? Should they give the child up for adoption?

What's the lie that John and Karen believed that caught them by surprise?

_____

_____

_____

_____

_____

Why didn't God protect John and Karen from an unplanned pregnancy? After all, they did not actually have intercourse and they wanted to please God with their lives.

_____

_____

_____

_____

_____

If you are dating someone, what type of sexual activity can you engage in that will keep you safe and will also be pleasing to God?

_____

_____

_____

_____

_____

The Gospel Truth

Believing the lie that God will protect you from the negative consequences of sin is nothing new. People are easily led astray by self-proclaimed prophets who preach an easy message of safety when, in reality, circumstances are far from safe.

More than 3,500 years ago, the prophet Jeremiah undressed a similar lie for the people of Israel. God's message was simple:

Follow My commands and you will be blessed. Problems arose, however, when the people of Israel grew weary of God's ways and started devising their own. People today fall into the same trap. When we start living on our own and for ourselves, we often want others to join us, so we create lies to convince ourselves and others that it's safe to turn away from God.

The king and the priests in Jeremiah's day were preaching the lie of "safe religion." "Safe religion" says you can do what you want during the week as long as you go to church and ask for forgiveness. You don't need to worry about the consequences of sin, because God will always forgive you, always love you and always protect you, even when you totally disobey His commands.

The people of Israel felt safe because they had the temple. Some believed that God actually lived in the temple and that if you were in the temple, you were "in with God." Others believed that because God called a former king, Solomon, to build the temple, God would never allow His temple to be destroyed.

Believers in "safe religion" look to churches and pastors to tell them they are "safe" even when they are not. "Safe religion" says that it's easier to do your own thing than to follow God.

But because God loves us, He doesn't let us wander away from Him without giving a warning. Jeremiah openly undressed this lie of safe religion.

Read Jeremiah 7:1-11.

If you were Jeremiah, what feelings would you have if you sensed God telling you to go tell the people that they were believing a lie?

_____

_____

_____

Verse four reads, "Don't trust in deceptive words that say, 'This is the temple . . .'" Jeremiah was speaking against the other "prophets" of that day who used deceptive words and told the people that they were safe.

How do you know who to listen to? We have modern-day prophets who preach a message of "safe sex." How do you determine whether those words are true or not?

_____

_____

_____

_____

_____

_____

Read Jeremiah 7:12-15.

What consequences would the people experience because they believed the lie of safety instead of following God's way of life?

_____

_____

_____

_____

_____

Can you think of a time when you suffered negative consequences because you believed a lie? What were the consequences?

_____

_____

_____

_____

_____

Read 1 Samuel 4:1-11.

People reacted violently to Jeremiah's message. They did not want to hear that they were not safe. Jeremiah 26:7-9 records how people reacted to Jeremiah's sermon, which undressed the lie of "safe religion."

If you know someone who regularly engages in "safe sex," do you think they want to know the truth about the dangers of safe sex? Why or why not?

_____

_____

_____

Often we value our own desires over the truth and believe that what we don't know can't hurt us. We choose to believe those who tell us what we want to hear.

A wise, old man named Solomon wrote the book of Proverbs. Solomon had it all: money, fame, power and, yes, multiple partners. The Bible describes Solomon as a man who had 700 wives and 300 sex slaves. If anyone in the Bible could comment on the power of sex in one's life, it would indeed be Solomon.

Check out these words from the book of Proverbs, which is a collection of Solomon's thoughts about life.

Drink water from your own cistern, running water from your own well. Should your springs overflow in the streets, your streams of water in the public square? Let them be yours alone, never to be shared by strangers. May your fountain be blessed, and may you rejoice in the wife of your youth. A loving doe, a graceful deer—may her breasts satisfy you always, may you ever be captivated by her love. Why be captivated, my son, by an adulteress? Why embrace the bosom of another man's wife?

For a man's ways are in full view of the Lord, and he examines all his paths. The evil deeds of a wicked man ensnare him; the cords of his sin hold him fast. He will die for lack of discipline, led astray by his own great folly (Proverbs 5:15-23).

If Solomon were leading this lesson, what advice do you think he would give you about sex?

_____

_____

_____

_____

_____

_____

When you think back to the activity in lesson three, would it be easier or harder to rejoice in the "wife of your youth" (or husband of your youth) if you discovered that she or he had an STD? What about if you had to tell your spouse that you had an STD?

_____

_____

_____

_____

How can a lack of discipline, when it comes to sexuality, lead to death?

_____

_____

_____

_____

Doing the Truth

After reviewing your answers to the quiz, take a moment to answer the following questions on your own:

What information did you learn from the video that was new to you?

_____

_____

_____

_____

_____

How does this impact your thinking about the concept of safe sex?

_____

_____

_____

_____

_____

If you were to ask God for advice about safe sex, what do you think He would say?

_____

_____

_____

_____

_____

As you come to the end of this lesson, take some time as a group to complete this T-Chart to describe the negative consequences of using condoms and other contraceptives as a means to have "safe sex."

Negative Consequences	Positive Consequences

SESSION 4

The Big Finish

In the video, Lakita mentions that condoms are not able to protect your emotions, relationships and psychological well-being.

Describe the negative effects that having sex with someone can have on your emotions.

_____

_____

_____

_____

Describe how having sex outside of marriage could be damaging to your relationship with your friends, your family and God.

_____

_____

_____

_____

Is there really anything safe about "safe sex"? No. Is there really anything safe about following God's pattern for sex? Yes.

Note
1. While John and Karen are not their real names, the couple gave permission for this part of their story to be shared.

They're Going to Do It Anyway

Introduction

Ben never saw it coming.

His girlfriend, Shannon, called and asked him to come over because she had something important to talk to him about. As a senior in high school, Ben's friends were impressed that he had a girlfriend who was 22 years old. They did things that his friends only experienced in their dreams. Ben stopped going to his youth group because work and his new girlfriend took a lot of time.

When Shannon called, he figured the relationship was over. Shannon had been pretty moody lately and Ben couldn't figure out why. When he walked into her room (in her mom's house), she said, "I just took a pregnancy test. I'm pregnant. What do you think we should do?"

Later that week when Ben told his parents, they asked him, "How could you let this happen?"

He responded, "Hey, it's not my fault. It just happened. Really, it's nobody's fault. I didn't want this, but I guess God had other plans."

Ben believed the lie that having a baby was out of his control. After all, sometimes things just happen. Right?

Wrong. Sex doesn't just happen. God gave us a desire to enjoy sex. But pregnancy, STDs and broken hearts happen because we choose to satisfy our desires outside of God's plan while ignoring the possible consequences.

In this lesson, we will undress two lies:

1. "They're going to do it anyway because sex is an uncontrollable body function."
2. "It just happened."

The Naked Truth with Lakita

As you prepare to listen to Lakita, ask God in prayer to use this time to help you gain wisdom for the choices you make in your life.

As you watch the video, be sure to write down your thoughts and questions.

The Hook-Up

Safe sex just isn't safe. Condoms and other contraceptives cannot guarantee protection against STDs or pregnancy. The condom companies know that, educators know that and now you know that.

So why do so many people promote safe sex? Basically, people have a very low expectation of your ability to control your desire. Adults who couldn't or don't control their urges don't think you can either.

The lie of safe sex continues to thrive because people argue, "Since teenagers are going to do it anyway, we need to teach them how to have sex in the safest possible manner."

To help you consider the logic of that thinking, consider what you would think if you were the parent of a middle school student, and your son came home to tell you this story about health class:

We had the D.A.R.E. (Drug Abuse Resistance Education) officer in class today. It was great. As part of the demonstration, the officer asked Bobby to come to the front. He had Bobby hold out his arm and make a fist, and then he rolled up Bobby's sleeve and tied a rubber tube around his bicep. He turned to the class and said, "Okay, class, this is a syringe. I want to show you how much heroin you can put into your arm before you overdose. We know that you will most likely do drugs anyway, so we want to be sure you are safe. The nurse will have clean needles at the end of class for those of you who might need them this weekend."

As a parent, if you were to talk to the D.A.R.E. officer who taught that class, what would you say? Or what would you think if you were sitting in your civics class and the teacher said this:

We live in a very violent culture. Kids carry guns to school. Sometimes, the really crazy students actually go on rampages and start shooting innocent victims. Since you will probably become violent yourself, we want to show you how to properly use a handgun and how to wear a bullet-proof vest. We are going to make these guns and vests available at the counselor's office, so if you have the desire to be violent, you can first talk to an adult who understands. We won't judge you or tell your parents, but we do want you to be safe.

What do you think? Is it inevitable that every student will be violent? Is the best way to keep them safe to show them how to use a gun and vest?

Of course not! But that's exactly the lie that is told to students all over the country when it comes to teaching an abstinent lifestyle. Students across the country are taught the lie "You're going to do it anyway" with regard to sex. Because educators, government officials and other adults believe students cannot control their sexual urges, they think the best they can do is to show teenagers how to protect themselves.

The Bible teaches that you *can* control your desires, that you *can* have discipline in your actions, and that if you wait for the right time and place (after you say "I do"), you will enjoy incredible satisfaction. As Lakita says, "I do you, you do me and we don't do nobody else."

The Bible does not treat people as animals. Instead, the Bible portrays us as people with free will who, with God's help, can control our desires. How do you stay sexually pure? Make a decision and stick to it!

You see, many people feel like sex just happens. You may not intend to have sex, but one thing leads to another and next thing you know, you wake up wondering if you will be late for your next period (and I don't mean class).

The Gospel Truth

The lie "They're going do it anyway" is nothing new. People have been trying to convince others to turn away from God's plan for sex in almost every culture since the beginning of time. It's important to know God's wisdom on the matter. Like God, educators and doctors tell us that abstinence is the best way to avoid negative consequences—but they immediately follow up with facts with an insistence to "use protection" because *they're going to do it anyway*. God has higher expectations for you than our culture does. The Bible sets the standard for great sex, and it doesn't look anything like haphazard sex with many partners.

Wisdom, by definition, is putting knowledge into action. Some people are book smart, but they don't apply what they know intellectually to their lives. That's not wisdom. Some people are street smart, but they don't apply what they've experienced to their lives. That's not wisdom, either. Finally, some people are Bible smart. They've read the Book and then applied God's Word to their experience. That's wisdom: taking the knowledge God has given and applying it to everyday life.

Solomon was a wise man. In fact, the Bible says he was one of the wisest men to have ever lived. You may remember Solomon from our last lesson: He was the guy with 700 wives and 300 concubines. It is true that he was wise, but he wasn't wise all the time. He did not always put his knowledge into action.

Solomon believed that it was possible for people to control their body's desires. He knew that it was not inevitable that people would have sex. In fact, he gave advice about how to deal with people who were trying to convince others to have sex.

Read Proverbs 5:1-6.

When Solomon wrote this proverb, he knew that there are people who tempt others to have sex by using smooth speech or their good looks. Young women encounter older guys who try to seduce them with smooth words or with their money and looks. Or young men are confronted by women who dress provocatively and sound sexy, making it difficult for the guy to think about anything aside from sex.

In the Bible, an adulteress was a woman who tried to convince a man to have sex with her outside of marriage. Solomon used images of the adulteress's lips dripping with honey and her speech being smooth like butter. Her words are sweet and smooth, just like the seductive men and women we just talked about.

Check out these questions to get you thinking wisely about the ways people might coerce you into sexual temptation:

What phrases or words do people use in order to convince someone to have sex?

_____

_____

_____

_____

What do you think Solomon meant when he wrote, "but in the end she is bitter gall, sharp as a double-edged sword"?

_____

_____

_____

_____

Do you know of a situation when someone was smooth-talked into having sex? Describe how that person felt about himself or herself because he or she gave in.

_____

_____

_____

_____

Check out verse six: "She gives no thought to the way of life; her paths are crooked, but she knows it not." The adulteress does not ponder the path and does not know that the way is unstable.

Does this proverb settle for the lie "They're going to do it anyway"?

_____

_____

_____

_____

What difference would it make if everyone was taught that having sex is not inevitable but is a choice?

_____

_____

_____

_____

Read Proverbs 5:7-14.

Sex does not just happen. People have sex because they take small and big steps in that direction. In verse eight, Solomon gave this advice about sexual temptation: "Keep to a path far from her, do not go near the door of her house."

Why would Solomon tell us to not even go near her house? In what ways do people start walking along the path of having sex long before they actually do the deed?

_____

_____

_____

_____

When you consider the end of your life, how do you want to look back on your sex life? Do you want to have regrets?

_____

_____

_____

Now let's address the second lie in this session: "It just happened." Does sex just happen?

Some accidents just happen. If you sit at a red light and someone plows into the back of your car, an accident "just happened." One minute you were fine, the next minute you were in a hospital bed.

Is sex like an accident? Or are there things we do and words we say that lead us down the path toward sex before marriage? Before Lakita tells us about the PIL, take a moment to reconsider the story of David and Bathsheba. (You may remember them from our first lesson.) Consider what things David did long before Bathsheba got pregnant that led them down the path.

Read 2 Samuel 11:1-5.

What six actions did David take that led him down the path of having sex with Bathsheba?

_____

_____

_____

_____

What could David had done that would have stopped the progression toward Bathsheba's pregnancy? Could Bathsheba have done anything?

_____

_____

_____

_____

Doing the Truth

In the video, Lakita talks about how sex involves the whole person and how it is so much more than two persons getting physical pleasure from one another. She mentions some of the negative impacts of not delaying your sexual gratification and not waiting for marriage. For example:

• Depression and suicide rates increase when young people are involved in regular sexual activity.

- Couples often break-up once they become sexually active with each other.
- Sex costs money when you need to get tested and treated for an STD.
- There are huge negative impacts on children who are raised in single-parent homes and in two-parent homes when parents have not completed their education.
- Supporting single moms and their children has significant cost to communities.

So, that's what is at stake if you don't wait until marriage. But what might you gain by remaining abstinent? Is there anything positive about practicing the abstinent lifestyle before marriage?

The Big Finish

The 12 Steps to Intimacy

A behavioral scientist named Desmond Morris studied numerous couples and found patterns that determined why some couples stay together for life and why some divorce. The amount of time spent bonding between important stages of intimacy during courtship became a kind of predictor of whether the relationship would succeed or fail. Couples who rushed through these steps or phases usually didn't have as strong a bond and were far more likely to divorce. The 12 Steps to Intimacy are as follows:

1. *Eye to Body:* This step is usually the first contact and usually passes very quickly because it is that point at which initial evaluations are made.

2. *Eye to Eye:* Eye contact and mutual acknowledgement is made at this stage. Each person knows that the

other has seen him or her and flirting or friendship might begin.

3. *Voice to Voice:* Two people begin talking and discover similar interests, opinions or values. But over time the nature of each other's character is revealed. Casual contact may also be made.

By the time you make it to Step 3, you should have figured out something about the nature of the other person's true character. Do you have a set of shared values, goals, interests or morals? Here is where you might decide to remain friends, or you might decide to court. If you prefer the term "date," then remember that the purpose of dating is to gather enough data to make a wise decision.

4. *Hand to Hand:* Holding hands is the point at which the relationship advances to the first non-casual, non-threatening, body contact. Levels of trust deepen from simple friendship because a physical line has been crossed. Up until this point, disengagement may be "pain-free" because there has been no commitment or expectation beyond friendship.

5. *Arm to Shoulder:* There still is a sense of space between partners while holding hands, but an arm around the shoulder of another person signifies a deepening closeness and intimacy.

6. *Arm to Waist:* Arm to waist indicates growing comfort and familiarity, and this step also makes a statement of escalating feelings.

By this point you should have decided whether or not this courtship should advance to engagement or marriage, or return to being friends so as not to cause further relational bonding.

7. *Mouth to Mouth:* Mouth-to-mouth kissing is very significant in the process because it is at this point that the steps can rapidly accelerate. Full frontal embrace often follows. Mouth to mouth kissing is often preceded by (1) mouth to hand, (2) mouth to cheek or forehead, and/or (3) a peck on the lips.

8. *Hand to Head:* Touching another's head is a sign of deepening trust and is highly intimate, partially because so many vital senses are concentrated in the head.

Many who have chosen abstinence choose this point as the line beyond which only married couples engage (though I chose between point six and point seven as my line before I got married).

9. *Hand to Body:* Hand to body is where foreplay begins because it is usually to a part of the body that is not publicly exposed.

10. *Mouth to Breast:* Mouth to breast obviously suggests at least partial nudity is involved. Here foreplay continues and emotions are running high.

11. *Hand to Genitals:* Hand to genitals is quite intimate to say the least and is a major act of bonding.

12. *Sexual Intercourse:* Intense bonding like this is ultimately intended for two individuals committed for life in a marriage relationship.

If you build a relationship on steps one through six, you will have a much stronger foundation for marriage. Once you begin mouth-to-mouth kissing, verbal communication lessens and "the point of no return" approaches rapidly.

If you were a parent of a teenager, where would you want your kid to stop? What stop do you think would be God's best for your future son or daughter?

_____

_____

_____

_____

_____

_____

_____

_____

What about you? Where do you think God calls you to establish a boundary? What is the best way to approach physical intimacy and relationships?

_____

_____

_____

_____

_____

_____

_____

_____

_____

Everybody's Doing It

Introduction

In a 2005 issue of *CosmoGirl*, there is a photo of a girl approaching a guy carrying a box of condoms and a can of whipped cream. The caption reads, "Sophia's got Chad totally whipped."[1]

What images come to your mind when you think about that ad? Are you thinking about Thanksgiving dinner and whipped cream on pumpkin pie? Not likely. You may be grossed out or subtly intrigued, but either way you are thinking about sex. You've been influenced, even if in just a small way, by the words on the page. Is it possible to see that ad and not at least have a passing thought about sex?

The fact is, the more you hear and see images and words about sex, the more you become curious about sex. Why? God made you to want and enjoy sex. You were created as a spiritual being with sexual desires.

In the October 2006 issue of *Seventeen Magazine,* these three articles are back to back:

1. Is Your Life at Risk? Here are health facts smart girls like you might not know. (Three of the four "risks" give a clear message of the danger of "unsafe sex.")

2. Why He Doesn't Turn You On: Not into hooking up with your guy? Here are some common reasons why that may be the case. (This article helps girls to understand why they don't get excited about sex with their boyfriends.)

3. Condoms 101: What you need to know. Even if you're not having sex, learning about condoms will make sure you're safe when it's time. (This article includes facts on "safe sex," including drawings on how to put a condom on a penis as well as a warning that the only way to 100 percent guarantee you won't get pregnant is not to have sex.)

These articles are intended to help girls be safe and to help them feel better about themselves, but they also present the most potent, powerful and deceptive lie dressed up in truth's clothing: the lie that "Everybody's doing it."

Seventeen Magazine is no different than many music videos, movies, television shows, and many of our friends, parents and other adults who not only believe but perpetuate the lie that everybody is either having sex or will have sex sometime before they are married.

In this lesson we'll undress that lie as well as the lie "I just listen to the beat."

Before we jump into the lesson, let's do a quick review of what we've learned so far.

The Naked Truth with Lakita

As you prepare to listen to Lakita, ask God in prayer to use this time to help you gain wisdom about the choices you are making in your life.

As you watch the video, be sure to write down your thoughts and questions.

_____

_____

_____

_____

_____

_____

_____

_____

_____

The Hook-Up

Popular music and other media influences would have us believe the lie that "Everybody's doing it." But is it true? *Is everybody doing it?* Let's take a quick survey and then do a little science experiment to find out.

Short and Sweet Survey
(circle one)

What percentages of high school students have had sex before graduating high school?
   a. less than 25%
   b. 25% to 49%
   c. 50% to 74%
   d. 75%

Of those who have had sex, what percentage wish they had waited?
   a. less than 25%
   b. 25% to 49%
   c. 50% to 74%
   d. 75%

What are the pressures *from the outside* that cause young people to have sex before marriage, to drink, to do drugs or to behave in other ways that have negative consequences?

Media

_____

_____

Peer pressure (e.g., to be popular you have to have sex)

_____

_____

Boyfriend or girlfriend

_____

_____

What are the pressures *on the inside* of a person that help him or her overcome those outside pressures?

The Holy Spirit

_____

_____

Boundaries that you have set

_____

_____

Respect for yourself and the principles that you have established for your life

_____

_____

Respect for the other person and respect for your future mate

_____

_____

_____

Respect for your religious beliefs

_____

_____

Respect for your parents

_____

_____

The Gospel Truth

The Bible has a lot to say about how we are influenced by our friends, and suggests that what we listen to has a big impact on the ways we think and act.

The psalms are a great example of the kinds of words we should fill our minds with—it is a great worship book. The psalms tell about God and about people. David, the guy who got Bathsheba pregnant because he didn't control his sexual urges, wrote many psalms that are included in the Bible. David understood both how to follow God and what situations can turn us away from God.

Read Psalm 1.

The Bible uses the word "blessed" to describe someone who is content, happy and feeling extremely good in his or her soul. To be blessed is to be close to God and to enjoy the people and events God has placed in your life. This passage describes what you should and should not do in order to experience God's blessing.

According to this psalm, what do you need to avoid if you want to be blessed?

_____

_____

_____

This psalm describes a pattern of bad influences, which slowly becomes a part of your life. First, you walk with the idea of doing something. Second, you stand and follow the way of a bad idea. And finally, you embrace it by sitting and staying awhile with bad influences. The more you hang out with "bad counsel" the greater influence it will have over you.

In what ways do you see Christians "walking with" the idea of having sex long before they actually have sex?

_____

_____

_____

According to this psalm, what should you do in order to feel blessed?

_____

_____

_____

When you think about how you spend your time, what you read, what you see on television or at the movies, do you think you get more messages from God's Word about sexuality or more messages from other "counsel"?

_____

_____

_____

Doing the Truth

Let's do some sexual research of our own. Sound good?

In your small group, study the lyrics of three songs given to you by your group leader. After reading the lyrics together, answer the following questions:

What's the basic message about sex in this song?

_____

_____

_____

Does this particular song encourage or discourage the message of abstinence?

_____

_____

_____

Lakita tells us that the best way to be successful in a decision to remain abstinent is to begin with the end in mind, make a plan and then find others who will support you. If Lakita hadn't known what she really wanted in the end, she could have been crushed at the commercial shoot. But she knew the end she had in mind for herself.

The fact is that not everybody is doing it, and for those who *have* done it, many regret that they ever did. If they had planned ahead with the end in mind, they might not have those regrets.

Below is a list of scenarios that you might face sometime in your life. Take some time to decide in advance what you might do in these situations. In the discussion time after this exercise, take some time to talk about situations that you've already encountered or have heard about from others.

What would you do if:

Your boyfriend or girlfriend asks you to go spend time at his/her home when no one else is there

_____

_____

_____

You arrive at a boyfriend or girlfriend's house and discover that no one else is home

_____

_____

_____

_____

You're at a party where people are drinking and your date offers you a drink

_____

_____

_____

_____

You've been dating a person for three months and he/she tells you that he/she believes that you're ready to have sex

_____

_____

_____

_____

After you've had a chance to write your responses, develop some strategies as a group that might work if you found yourself in those situations.

The Big Finish

One of the first things the Holy Spirit told Lakita when she became a Christian as a teenager was, "You will be seen by the eyes of millions, but you are to perform for an audience of One." God is that audience of One. When you place God first, you'll find that the desire to please Him will far outweigh any pressure you feel from the outside. When God comes first, you'll be like the full, unopened soda can, not crushed by the influence of friends, the media or even your own passions.

The apostle Paul knew a lot about the pressure to conform to the world and the ability that God has to transform our minds to resist those pressures. He wrote:

> I appeal to you therefore, [brothers and sisters], by the mercies of God, to present your bodies as a living and holy sacrifice, acceptable to God, which is your spiritual service of worship. Do not be conformed to this world, but be transformed by the renewing of your minds, so that you may discern what is the will of God, that which is good and acceptable and perfect (Romans 12:1-2, *NASB*).

What can you do to place God first and to present your body to Him as an act of worship?

_____

_____

_____

Describe how a person would live if they had a renewed mind that knew God's will.

_____

_____

_____

When you are focused on God and what He thinks about you, then it doesn't matter what kind of pressure others put on you. You couldn't care less.

Note

1. Rebecca Grace, "Teen Magazines Send Mixed Messages," AgapePress, October 17, 2005. http://headlines.agapepress.org/archive/10/172005a.asp (accessed on November 16, 2006).

Marriage Is Just a Piece of Paper

Introduction

How fat do you have to be before it's too late to start dieting?

As a college student at Indiana University, Jared Fogle weighed 425 pounds. He was *huge*. He tried many diets but nothing worked, and at times he felt that—since he had gained so much weight—there was no point in dieting. After all, he had already blown it.

Jared then discovered the Subway sandwich and the rest is history. Jared lost over 230 pounds and now weights 190.[1] Before he discovered this new weight-loss solution, he was tempted to believe a lie that because he had made mistakes in his past, he couldn't make good decisions in the future. That's a lie that needs to be undressed.

Is it ever too late to start doing the right thing?

Nature, experience and God's Word all point to this simple truth: It's never too late.

- When a person stops smoking cigarettes, his or her lungs immediately start to heal.
- When a person begins an exercise program, the body begins to move almost immediately toward better health.
- When someone goes to counseling to deal with emotional problems, things often begin to change within the first few sessions.
- When someone has had sex and he or she makes a decision to stop and begin a life of abstinence, things begin to change physically, emotionally and spiritually.

If you've already had sex, if you've already had a baby, or if you've already contracted an STD, you might be thinking to yourself, *All this talk about abstinence is great for everyone else, but I've already blown it.*

We are going to undress that lie in this lesson. No matter what you've done, who you've done it with, or where you have done it, there are benefits in turning from your past and making a decision to honor God and respect yourself by remaining abstinent until marriage.

We will also talk about the benefits of waiting until marriage, and not just until you find the person you think you love. Another lie that ruins God's plan for an amazing sex life says, "Marriage is just a piece of paper." This lie dresses itself up as truth when people convince themselves that living together is the best way to get to know each other before signing a piece of paper. Unfortunately, experience proves that living together dramatically increases your risk of a broken relationship in the future.

The Naked Truth with Lakita

As you prepare to listen to Lakita, ask God in prayer to use this time to help you gain wisdom on choices you are making in your life.

As you watch the video, be sure to write down your thoughts and questions. Take a moment to talk with the group about your questions and comments after watching the video.

_____

_____

_____

_____

_____

_____

The Hook-Up

While more than half of high school students have not had sex, more than 40 percent have had sex. Of that 40 percent, two-thirds wished they had waited. Maybe you are still considering whether or not you want to embrace the abstinent lifestyle, and you're wondering if it really makes a difference.

Check out what singer-songwriter Kim Hill has to say about sex outside of marriage:

> The decision to have sex outside of marriage results in a slow, subtle kind of death. It's the death of innocence and purity. The shattering of dreams. The numbing of a once vibrant, youthful spirit. The word abstinence implies denial and all sorts of negative restrictions. In truth, though, abstinence means wholeness and freedom and peace. A life of virtue can be a difficult road, but it's a road of promise and excellence, and one without regret.[2]

Do you agree that sex outside of marriage results in a slow, subtle death of innocence and purity? Why or why not?

_____

_____

_____

If you choose an abstinent lifestyle, will you always feel peaceful and free, even when you are tempted to have sex or are hassled by others about your decision? Why or why not?

_____

_____

_____

_____

Let marriage be held in honor by all, and let the marriage bed be kept undefiled; for God will judge the fornicators and adulterers (Hebrews 13:4).

Throughout this study we've been talking about waiting to have sex until you are married. The passage from Hebrews 13:4 states clearly that God calls us to hold marriage in high esteem. Marriage according to God is a great thing.

Marriage has gotten a bad rap lately. Many people get divorced, which makes marriage seem like a bunch of empty promises. The marriage license seems like just another piece of paper and *feeling* like you are in love has become more important than signing "just a piece of paper." After all, can't you still be fully committed to someone without being married?

What do you think? Is living together in a committed relationship just like marriage?

Now here's a quick quiz that compares marriage to living together. Circle True or False for each statement.

1. Living together before getting married helps you prepare for marriage, and couples who live together first have happier, stronger marriages.
   True   False

2. People who are married are more likely to experience domestic violence than couples who live together.
   True   False

3. Children raised in a home where the mother is living with someone other than the children's father are more likely to be abused and molested.
   True   False

4. Couples who are married have sex more often and have more satisfying sex lives than couples who are not married.
   True   False

5. Couples who live together before marriage are more likely to cheat on their spouses after they marry.
   True   False

6. Couples who live together have the lowest level of relational satisfaction compared to all other premarital living arrangements.
   True   False

7. Couples that marry as opposed to simply living together live longer and healthier lives.
   True   False

The Gospel Truth

During the past six weeks, we've seen some pretty dramatic consequences of sex outside of marriage. STDs, unwanted pregnancy, broken relationships and loss of innocence are all good reasons to abstain from sex outside of marriage.

Perhaps the most compelling reason why the Christian should practice abstinence is that it pleases God. God's plan for you is that you experience amazing sex within the context of marriage. That's not only God's plan; it is also God's command.

One of God's Top Ten Ways to Healthy Living (most people call this the Ten Commandments) reads, "Thou shall not commit adultery." Adultery simply means having sex with someone who is not your husband or wife. In fact, Moses, who received these commandments, also received this command:

If a man commits adultery with another man's wife—
with the wife of his neighbor—both the adulterer and
the adulteress must be put to death (Leviticus 20:10).

Death for sex! Can you imagine what would happen if that
law were instituted in the United States? Safe sex would take on
a whole new meaning. For the ancient Israelites, there were no
second chances for people caught in the act of adultery.

When Jesus came along, He offered an alternative to how
the religious leaders interpreted God's commands. The religious
leaders of His day emphasized punishment. While Jesus never
diminished the importance of following God's commands, He
emphasized grace over punishment.

In other words, everyone gets a second chance.

Read John 8:1-11.

How do you think the woman felt when she was caught in the
act of adultery? What about when the men surrounded her and
were ready to kill her? If she was caught in the act, where is the
guy she was with?

_____

_____

_____

_____

How do you think the crowd felt when they demanded that
Jesus pronounce judgment on the woman and instead He sat
on the ground and wrote in the sand?

_____

_____

_____

_____

_____

_____

Jesus offered an alternative to the religious leaders who were ready to condemn. Jesus simply followed the pattern of second chances that God revealed throughout the Old Testament. Remember David, the king who slept with another man's wife and then had that man killed? God gave him a second chance.

Read 2 Samuel 12:13-14.

What was David's response to God when his sin was found out?

_____

_____

_____

_____

How did God respond to David?

_____

_____

_____

_____

Read 2 Samuel 12:24-25.

How did God respond to David and Bathsheba after they had experienced the drastic consequences of their sin (the death of their child)?

_____

_____

_____

_____

Did God give them an opportunity to start over? Would God give you an opportunity to start over?

_____

_____

_____

_____

David wrote Psalm 51 in response to his sin with Bathsheba. David's psalm serves as a model prayer for those who have not followed God's plan of abstinence. It also gives great insight into how God views someone who has turned away from Him.

Read Psalm 51:1-12.

Write down the words or phrases that are the most meaningful to you when you think about starting over with God.

_____

_____

_____

_____

Read Psalm 51:13-19.

Complete the following sentence: "The ways that David plans to live differently in response to God's forgiveness are . . ."

_____

_____

_____

_____

The fact is that everyone sins. In some way, we all turn away from God and do our own thing. Jesus came to draw us back to God. Jesus is God's way of reaching the whole world to bring us all back into a close relationship with Him.

You may know people who claim to be Christians but don't want to live in the way God desires. God wants true believers. God's plan for you is to be "in Christ." In other words, God wants Jesus Christ to live in you. That happens when we simply ask the Lord to forgive us of past sins and to take control of our lives. Now check out this amazing verse from 2 Corinthians 5:17-18:

> Therefore, if anyone is in Christ, he is a new creation; the old has gone, the new has come! All this is from God, who reconciled us to himself through Christ and gave us the ministry of reconciliation.

★   ★   ★

Well, it's time to undress another lie. Living together looks good. In fact, living together seems like the best of all possible worlds: convenient sex, steady companionship, and if things go bad you can just walk away. But that's the problem. If you know that someone could walk away, it's impossible to fully give yourself to anyone.

Nobody likes to be alone. God did not create us to be alone. In fact, when God made the world, everything was good except for one thing: The man was originally on his own. When you commit yourself to someone for a lifetime, that commitment makes it possible to truly know someone.

Read Genesis 2:18-24.

What does this passage say about God's plan for men and women?

_____

_____

_____

_____

Why would God say that it's important to leave your mother and father behind and let your marriage commitment be the primary commitment?

_____

_____

_____

_____

_____

_____

_____

Is it possible to be completely committed to more than one person?

_____

_____

_____

_____

_____

_____

_____

Doing the Truth

Let's take a moment to use the following T-Chart to talk about the positive value of secondary virginity. Make a list of all the positive consequences that someone can experience if he or she chooses an abstinent lifestyle after he or she has had sex, has contracted an STD, or has had a baby. In the same column, list the positive impact an abstinent lifestyle could have on your relationship with God.

Don't forget to also make a list of the negative consequences of continuing to be sexually active. Again, how would being sexually active impact your walk with Christ?

Negative Consequences	Positive Consequences

Five Steps to Becoming a Secondary Virgin

1. Make a firm commitment to save yourself for marriage from now on, and believe you can do it. (Because you can!)

2. Get away from people, places, things and situations that weaken your self-control. Sometimes the healthiest thing we can do is to avoid people who tempt us.

3. Avoid intense hugging, passionate kissing and anything else that leads to lustful thoughts and behavior. Anything beyond a brief, simple kiss can quickly become dangerous.

4. Find non-physical ways to show your love and appreciation.

5. Remember that anyone can start over, including you! When you focus on commitment and self-discipline, you can control your impulses.[3]

The Big Finish

Take a few minutes to reflect on the following passages of Scripture. Be sure to jot down any words or phrases that stand out to you as you read, especially as each passage relates to what you read about or heard in today's session.

Romans 5:8

_____

_____

_____

_____

Romans 6:23

_____

_____

_____

_____

_____

Romans 8:1

_____

_____

_____

_____

Romans 8:38-39

_____

_____

_____

_____

_____

Romans 10:9

_____

_____

_____

_____

_____

Notes

1. "Jared's Statistics." http://www.subway.com (accessed on September 25, 2006).
2. "Celebrity Quotes on Saving Sex for Marriage." http://www.lovematters.com (accessed on September 25, 2006).
3. "Five Steps to Becoming a Secondary Virgin." http://www.lovematters.com/star tover.htlm (accessed on September 18, 2006).

Make a Decision, Make a Commitment

Introduction

You may remember this story as told by Lakita in our first video session:

When I was 11 years old, during my family's annual visit to Alabama, I woke up to discover that my grandfather was nowhere to be found. After a few days, I realized that his disappearance was a daily occurrence. So one afternoon, I decided to wait for him out on the porch. When he finally came back, I asked him, "Granddaddy, where do you go in the mornings?"

"I go to talk to my best friend," he answered.

"Who's that?" I asked.

"Your grandmother," he answered.

Now, my grandmother had been dead for four or five years. But six days a week, excluding Sundays—which was his day of rest—my grandfather would get up while it was still dark and walk down the dirt road with his cane. He loved to make the two-mile journey to his daily destination—our family cemetery—just as the sun was coming up. He would sit in his lounge chair next to her headstone for hours. Then he'd walk two miles back home. He was 90 years old.

"Why do you do this?" I asked.

"Because Ada was my best friend," he said, and started to tear up. "That woman made me feel like I could

take over the world. You know, there's nothing I wouldn't
have done for her."

As we sat on the porch that morning, my granddaddy told me all kinds of stories about he and my grandmother: how she waited for him to come back from WWI,
how she helped spare him from being lynched, and how
they got their family through the Great Depression. He
also took time to tell me that the first time he ever kissed
my grandmother was when the minister said, "You may
now kiss the bride."

They were married more than 60 years and raised
12 children together. So it was obvious that after they
said "I do" . . . they did.

The last thing my granddaddy said is the thing that
I still remember the most from our entire conversation:
"You know, I don't know anything about any other
woman and I don't want to, because Ada . . . well, she
was the stuff."

I remember taking a deep breath in awe. That's
what I wanted. I knew from that moment on that afternoon in Alabama that I wanted what my grandparents
had. I wanted to be like them and wait until I got married before I had sex . . .

Now my granddaddy didn't have more than a third-
grade education, and he didn't know anything about
safe sex. All he knew is that he loved this woman more
than life itself, and he was true to her throughout his
entire life. That was the vision he gave me at 11 years old
that helped me see abstinence as the means to reach the
desired end: a deep and lasting love.[1]

Lakita knew from a young age what she wanted to be when
she was 90. She took a long look at her life through her grand-

daddy's eyes and made a decision: She wanted God's best for her entire life, not just her sex life.

Lakita put into the practice the words of Psalm 90:

Teach us to number our days so that we might gain a heart of wisdom (Psalm 90:12).

Keeping the end of your life in mind will help you make wise decisions about how to live your life today. In this final lesson, we are going to review the core principles that have been presented throughout the previous seven sessions. You will be asked to consider the whole of your life and how the decisions you make today about your sex life will impact the rest of your life.

The Naked Truth with Lakita

As you prepare to listen to Lakita's final video session, ask God to use this time to help you gain wisdom about choices you are making in your life.

As you watch the video, review some of the core principles you have learned during this study in the space below.

1. The amount of time you are married is _____ times longer (on average) than the amount of time you will have to wait to have sex.

2. The best decision-making process is:

• Know your _____ and the _____.

• Make a decision. Choose an _____ and set a _____.

• Plan and take practical _____ to achieve your _____.

• Find _____ who will _____ you.

3. Write down some of the benefits and positive consequences of saving sex for marriage.

_____

_____

_____

_____

_____

4. Write down one way that Lakita's testimony encourages you to make a decision to choose God's plan for you to save sex for marriage.

_____

_____

_____

_____

_____

Take a moment to talk with the group about your questions and comments after watching the video.

The Hook-Up

In the 1992 Barcelona Olympics, the world witnessed an incredible example of determination to finish a race. Derek Redmond was ready for victory when he entered the semifinals for the 400m. Derek's running career had been peppered with injuries, but this year looked like his turn to go for the gold.

Derek got off to a clean start and was running smoothly when, about 150m into the race, his right hamstring muscle tore and he fell to the ground. When he saw the stretcher-bearers rushing towards him, he knew he had to finish the race. Redmond jumped up and began hobbling forward despite his pain. [2]

Suddenly from out of the crowd, a man in a T-shirt came and grabbed Derek. It was his father. Derek told his dad that he had to finish the race. Walking painfully and slowly, Derek finished the race with his father's support the entire way. Derek did not win a medal that day, but he went down in history as 65,000 screaming fans gave Derek and his father a standing ovation as they crossed the finish line.

Derek was able to complete the race because he never took his eyes off the finish line. For many decisions we make in life, we will never reach our goal if we only focus on what's immediately in front of us.

* * *

To get a picture of how important it is to look farther out than the end of your nose, place the handle of a broom in the palm of your hand and try to balance it while you look only at your palm.

Can you balance the broom?

Now change your focus. Without changing anything else, look up and focus on the bristle-end of the broom in the air.

Now can you balance the broom?

Your life is like the broom exercise: If you focus only on what is immediately in front of you, you won't be able to hold it together for the long term. However, if you begin by looking to the long-term future and then plan accordingly, you will be better prepared for success.

The Gospel Truth

Choosing not to have sex before you get married is pretty easy when you are sitting with a bunch of people who are like-minded. Youth groups and college groups around the country have classes and conferences just like this one, and at the end, people are asked to make a decision: Will you choose an abstinent lifestyle?

After all the positive reasons given for saving sex for marriage, and after all the negative reasons to avoid sex with more than one partner, people often make a decision to say, "Yes, I want to follow God's plan to save sex until marriage." The conference or class ends with tears, determination and joy for the decisions to follow God's will. But, choosing not to have sex before marriage is easy when you are in an atmosphere that promotes abstinence. It is the step *after* a commitment to abstinence that is tough.

The second step of the commitment occurs when you face your first real test:

You meet a really smart, cute and funny guy who sweeps you off your feet. You know he's The One, and he gently begins to push your boundaries. A little longer kiss, a slight touch between the legs when you are vulnerable, and suddenly you are swirling in a storm of indecision. Will you stay focused on your goal?

_____

_____

_____

_____

_____

_____

_____

You and a friend make a commitment together to stay pure until marriage. You decide to support each other. Your friend goes away for a weekend and later tells you that he went a little too far with someone at a party and ended up having oral sex. You are suddenly faced with a storm of emotions, including betrayal, anger and curiosity about what it must have felt like.

_____

_____

_____

_____

_____

_____

Or maybe you'll have an experience like Lakita when she was making the soda commercial. In a group of people, someone asks you about your sex life and when you say you are a virgin, you find yourself looking for help in the midst of a storm of people who are making fun of your resolve.

_____

_____

_____

_____

_____

_____

When you face a real test, what will you decide? Where will you find help?

One day, Jesus' disciples saw the most amazing thing: Jesus fed 5,000 people with just 5 loaves of bread and 2 fish. The disciples thought it would be impossible to feed that many people. After Jesus' miracle, they had a newfound respect for God's power. If Jesus could feed that many people with so little food, then anything was possible!

Immediately afterward, Jesus asked His disciples to get into a boat and go to the other side of the lake while He dismissed the crowd. After the crowds left, Jesus went up on a mountain to pray while the disciples paddled their boat across the lake.

A huge storm hit, and suddenly the disciples—who were so confident in God's power only hours before—forgot about Jesus' ability to save them. They were scared when they were thrown into a dangerous situation.

Read Matthew 14:22-33 to hear the story as told by one of the disciples who experienced the storm.

What did Jesus say to the disciples when they saw Him walking on the water? Why would He say that?

_____

_____

_____

_____

What happened when Peter took his eyes off of Jesus and focused on the storm?

_____

_____

_____

_____

_____

How did Jesus respond?

_____

_____

_____

_____

_____

Peter walked on water! He is one of only two people in history who was able to do that, and the other one is Jesus. How did Peter walk on water? *He decided to focus on Jesus and step out of the boat.*

Some people think being a virgin when you get married is impossible. But all things are possible when we keep our eyes on God and not on the storms that swirl around our lives.

If you choose to follow God's plan to save sex for marriage, what things can you do to keep your eyes on Jesus when you are in a storm of emotion, confusion or doubt?

_____

_____

_____

Read Matthew 6:25-34.

What does this passage say about God's ability to provide for your needs?

_____

_____

_____

What advice does Jesus give you so that you can stay focused on God?

_____

_____

_____

How does this passage speak to your needs for sex and God's provision?

_____

_____

_____

Doing the Truth

In our opening lesson, Lakita told a parable about two characters—Truth and Lie—who went skinny-dipping in the local pond. During the story, we learned that Lie stole Truth's clothes and wore them into town. Completely naked, Truth found Lie wearing his clothes and the two of them ended up in a heated discussion in front of the whole town. You, like the townspeople, are faced with a challenge: Will you believe a lie in truth's clothing or will you believe The Naked Truth?

Over the past seven weeks, we've undressed the following lies:

- "It can't happen to me."
- "I'll practice safe sex."
- "They're going to do it anyway."
- "Sex is an uncontrollable urge."
- "It just happened."
- "I just listen to the beat."
- "Everybody's doing it."
- "It's too late for me."
- "Marriage is just a piece of paper."

You've done a lot of work! Take some time to consider what you've experienced through this study by answering the following questions.

What did you learn that was surprising or new to you?

_____

_____

_____

_____

_____

_____

What is the most compelling reason that you heard for remaining sexually abstinent until marriage?

_____

_____

_____

_____

_____

What are your greatest challenges to remaining sexually abstinent until marriage?

_____

_____

_____

_____

_____

In what ways does your relationship with God impact your decision to remain abstinent until marriage?

_____

_____

_____

_____

_____

_____

★   ★   ★

"Teach us to number our days so that we might gain a heart of wisdom" (Psalm 90:12). If you choose to live your life with the end in mind, you can reach the goals you have set for yourself. Use the timeline on the following page to map out the hopes and dreams you have for your life. As you do this, ask God to give you wisdom as you number your days.

Birth

Elementary
School

High
School

High
School
Graduation

Death
Age 78

Here is a list of possible events and goals you might want to include on your timeline:

- Will you go to college? Graduate school?
- When will you start a job/career?
- Where will you live?
- Will you get married?
- When will you have kids? How many kids?
- When will you retire?
- When will you become a grandparent?

Take some time to talk about your dreams and hopes for your life with the entire group. After you have shared your dreams with the others in this study, use the worksheet below to develop a framework for your personal plan.

The Big Finish

It's one thing to have a dream or a goal in mind . . . it's another thing to know how to make your dreams become realities. You can begin to plan how to reach your goals right now, using the worksheet below. Fill in the blanks to start your plan.

Steps to Fulfilling Your Personal Plan

Step One: Write a specific goal for your life relating to your decision to remain abstinent until marriage.

_____

_____

_____

_____

_____

_____

_____

_____

_____

Example: Have a marriage like Lakita's grandparents.

Step Two: Identify people to support you in your plan.

_____

_____

_____

_____

_____

_____

_____

_____

Example: I want friends who want to be virgins when they get married, and I only want to date people with a similar goal.

Step Three: Make a list of concrete actions you can take to reach this goal.

_____

_____

_____

_____

_____

_____

_____

_____

Example: On the first date, let the person know my personal goals while I watch for their reaction. Avoid situations in which it would be tempting to have sex.

Step Four: Describe what you want in a mate. If you could design the perfect spouse, what would she/he look like? What kind of personality would she/he have? Would that person have faith? How many children would that person want? Where would she/he want to live? What kind of career would she/he have? Would that person be a virgin? Think of characteristics in a spouse that you would find ideal.

_____

_____

_____

_____

_____

_____

_____

_____

_____

Step Five: Start a letter to your future mate that you will give to him or her on your wedding day.

Dear future wife/husband,

_____

_____

_____

_____

_____

_____

_____

_____

_____

Lakita's Challenge

Our commitment to God is not a commitment if it is based on obligation, tradition or fear. When all is said and done, a commitment to God, parents, family, friends and future spouse will only last if it is rooted in deep devotion and love.

God desires the absolute best for us, and sometimes His best requires time, preparation and maturity. You must ask yourself if you love and trust Him enough to wait for His best, or if you love yourself and trust your own judgment more. Either way, there will be consequences—negative for the latter choice and positive for the former.

God created us to desire an intimate relationship with Him, and only He can fulfill our deepest desires. Today God offers you His love, presence and guidance. Will you choose to follow Him?

Notes
1. Lakita Garth, *The Naked Truth* (Ventura, CA: Regal Books, 2007), pp. 18-19.
2. "Derek Redmond: Finishing the Race." http://www.olympic.org/uk/athletes/profiles/bio (accessed September 27, 2006).

Journal

Journal

Why Wait?

In a world where it seems like "everybody's doing it," why should you say no to sex? Internationally known abstinence advocate and sought-after speaker Lakita Garth wants you to know that when you practice abstinence, you are making a decision that will change the course of your life.

Why wait?
Because you're worth it!

The Naked Truth Resources
Book • ISBN 978.08307.43285
Leader's Guide • ISBN 978.08307.43315
Student Guide • ISBN 978.08307.43308
DVD • UPC 607135.011032

More Relevant Resources from Regal

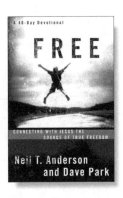
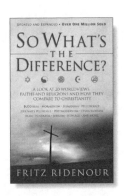
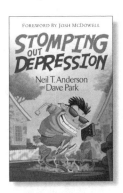